At Stego Books, we are committed to unlock your child's greatest potential. We aspire to equip every child with entrepreneurial and imperative soft skills essential to be leaders of tomorrow through storytelling.

Our books are designed by education and entrepreneurship experts to instill entrepreneurial spirit from a young age effectively.

We inspire purposeful reading every day!

www.stegobooks.com | Instagram: @stegolearning

Angela the Runner
Growth Mindset
How You Can Achieve Anything

Angela is a sweet little girl who loves running. One day, her school holds a sports day. Angela is excited to join the 100-meter race. She is eager to win the trophy.

"3, 2, 1, Go!" The referee shouts. Angela and the other racers start to run. With determination, Angela runs as fast as she can.

Unfortunately, Angela is the last person who finishes the race. The other racers run faster than her. Hence, Angela does not win the trophy.

With utter sadness, Angela begins to cry. She is disappointed to lose. With a broken heart, Angela goes back home empty-handed.

As Angela reaches home, her mom begins to comfort her. Her mom states, "Angela, even though you lost today, you can still win the trophy next time. You only need to have a secret key that unlocks your greatest potential."

With curiosity, Angela inquires, "What's the secret key, Mom?" Her mom smiles and responds, "By having a **Growth Mindset.** "

Mom further explains, "**Growth Mindset** begins from believing that anything is possible, and everything starts within you." Angela nods and carefully listens to what her mom says.

What should Angela say to build a **Growth Mindset**?
A. I'll never be able to run faster.
B. I can't run faster now, but I will eventually!

Angela's mom enthusiastically responds, "Correct, Angela! The first step to build a **Growth Mindset** is believing you will run faster eventually. You might not be able to immediately run faster today or tomorrow; however, with dedication, you will eventually!"

As the day turns into night, Angela prepares to sleep. Despite her sadness today, she is excited to take her first step of building a **Growth Mindset** starting tomorrow.

The next day, Angela begins practicing. With her stopwatch set, she is ready to improve her speed.

As Angela finishes her first practice run, she looks at her stopwatch, and she is disappointed. She does not improve her pace, and she wants to give up.

What should Angela say to build a **Growth Mindset**?
A. I will take a break and ask for help!
B. I have tried my best, and I just can not improve.

To build a **Growth Mindset**, seeking help from others to improve is vital. Thus, Angela calls her mother to improve her running skills and speed up her pace.

As Angela's mom comes to help her, she begins correcting Angela's running form. After listening to her mom's guidance carefully, Angela runs again.

Oh, no! Unfortunately, Angela suddenly slips and falls down. Angela becomes teary, and she is extremely sad. She feels that she always makes mistakes, and she can not progress any better.

What should Angela do to build a **Growth Mindset**?
A. Learn from her mistakes.
B. Dwell on her mistakes.

An important element of building a **Growth Mindset** is to not get disheartened when making mistakes. Consistently getting back up after falling down is essential to improve. Therefore, Angela learns from her mistakes.

As the sun sets, Angela goes back home and has dinner with her parents. She proudly tells her parents that she has learned from her mistakes, and she will keep on practicing daily to run faster.

With dedication, Angela consistently practices her running. Finally, she succeeds in achieving her fastest pace ever! She can't wait to tell her parents.

While having breakfast with her parents, Angela mentions she has achieved her goal; hence, she wants to stop practicing. Angela's mom encourages her to continue practicing as there is always room for improvement.

What should Angela do to build a **Growth Mindset**?
A. I have achieved my goal; thus, I will stop practicing.
B. I will continue practicing as there is always room for improvement.

"That's right, Angela!" Her mom declares. With a **Growth Mindset**, there is always an opportunity for growth, and there is no limit to anyone's potential.

With a bright smile on her face, Angela is thankful she has developed a **Growth Mindset** despite her setbacks. With a **Growth Mindset**, Angela is ready to improve even more.

A month passes by, and Angela's school holds another sports day. Angela is eager to join the 100-meter race again. She is confident of winning the trophy this time, as she has developed a **Growth Mindset** and enhanced her running skills.

"3, 2, 1, Go!" The referee shouts. Angela and the other racers begin to run. Fueled with a **Growth Mindset**, Angela runs and thrives.

With the biggest smile on her face, Angela wins the trophy! She scores first place in the race. She is extremely proud of her achievements.

As Angela reaches home, she immediately thanks her parents for teaching her the power of **Growth Mindset**. She hugs her parents tightly.

Angela is extremely happy as she has learned how to build a **Growth Mindset**. Angela confidently declares,"I can achieve anything with a **Growth Mindset!**"

What Goals Do You Want to Achieve With a Growth Mindset?

Growth Mindset Affirmations

I can achieve anything.

I will keep on practicing.

I embrace new challenges.

Nothing is impossible.

I strive to do my best.

Design Your Own Trophy!

Spot the 10 Differences!

Find the Hidden Words! 

A	T	G	R	O	W	T	H	S
B	C	T	R	O	P	H	Y	U
L	K	H	L	F	H	X	B	C
T	J	F	I	Q	B	Z	V	C
W	I	N	N	E	R	H	X	E
Y	H	Z	W	G	V	F	P	E
Q	M	I	N	D	S	E	T	D

1. Growth
2. Achieve
3. Trophy
4. Succeed
5. Winner
6. Mindset

Unjumble the Words!

Gnunnir

Eohss

Wtahcpsto

Nenirw

Cfoenitt

Nufsolewr

Spot the 10 Differences!

Find the Hidden Words!

A	T	G	R	O	W	T	H	S
B	C	T	R	O	P	H	Y	U
L	K	H	L	F	H	X	B	C
T	J	F	I	Q	B	Z	V	C
W	I	N	N	E	R	H	X	E
Y	H	Z	W	G	V	F	P	E
Q	M	I	N	D	S	E	T	D

1. Growth	3. Trophy	5. Winner
2. Achieve	4. Succeed	6. Mindset

Unjumble the Words!

Jumbled	Answer
Gnunnir	Running
Eohss	Shoes
Wtahcpsto	Stopwatch
Nenirw	Winner
Cfoenitt	Confetti
Nufsolewr	Sunflower

Angela the Runner
Growth Mindset
How You Can Achieve Anything